About The City

David Mudd

A PORTRAIT OF TRURO

BOSSINEY BOOKS

First published in 1979
by Bossiney Books
St Teath, Bodmin, Cornwall
Designed, typeset and printed in Great Britain by
Penwell Ltd, Parkwood, Callington,
Cornwall

©*David Mudd 1979*

ISBN 0 906456 20 7

PLATE ACKNOWLEDGMENTS

Cover photograph by Murray King
1, 5, 6, 10, 12-18, 29, 33, 42 Royal Institution of Cornwall
27, 37 John Crowther
2 Kerry Mudd
All other photographs by the author

INTRODUCTION

Although he has known Truro for much of his life, David Mudd admits that it's no easy task to write about Cornwall's only city.

'Truro's history,' he says, 'is more about the people who have lived there; the people who helped shape its growth and its way of life; and the people who — although born there — are now better known for their contribution to making life better, happier, and more useful in a much wider world than that bounded by the rivers Kenwyn and Allen.'

In getting down to writing this book, David Mudd rejected so obvious an opening as: 'In the beginning there were two rivers; and people lived in the land between those waters. They survived disease and built a town. In that town they built a great cathedral and the town became a city. And they called that city Truro.'

Similarly, he wanted to get away from the guidebook-ese of such gems as: 'Truro is just the picture of what one imagines a market town to be, old and quiet, permeated by the sound of running water which hurries down either side of the main street in a fresh, pure channel.'

About the City is, therefore, a more relaxed look at the story of Truro and its people. It tells of ancient charters; of the Civil War; of rivalry with Falmouth; of law and order; fun-fairs and funerals; of pills, policemen and stage-coaches. There are even fleeting glances at pirates and smugglers.

As David Mudd proves, it is not only 'fresh, pure, running water' that flows through Truro. A lively history and a unique atmosphere gush through its streets as well.

PROUD TRURO

Maiden aunts are surely the most fascinating and endearing rela-
tives of all. Outwardly they are prim — almost puritanical — yet a
secret grin, or a wink, suggests that they really know what mischief
is all about and were, perhaps, not exactly angels in their own child-
hood. They are always well dressed when visiting or being visited
yet, if caught unawares, are often found in well-tended but elderly
clothes.

Maiden aunts are ageless. In a short chat their conversation can
range from an intimate knowledge of all that is modern, to colourful
recollections of yesteryear.

Truro is Cornwall's maiden aunt. It is historic but not musty;
dignified but never dull; prosperous without vulgarity; and modern
without being brash.

There can be no disputing its great age. Certainly it existed as far
back as Roman days as some sort of settlement. It is, however,
bending history to claim — as the writer of one guide book did in the
1920s — that the development of Truro 'is of greatest interest and
goes back to the romantic age of the Celtic period when King Arthur
and his Knights of the Round Table fought a battle on the Strand of
Truro.'

Domesday Book, the survey of property earmarked for taxation
by William the Conqueror about 1086, suggests two settlements
named Great Truro and Little Truro, standing under a fortress.
This fortification was occupied by successive Earls of Cornwall and,
undoubtedly, was still very much a fact of life when Truro became
Cornwall's first chartered town in 1130 through a Royal recognition
which, when renewed in 1589, could refer to 'Proud Truro' in recognition of its seniority and dignity.

In the days of Edward I, in 1295, Truro's importance and status
was further underlined. Although it was controlled by Lords of the
Manor rather than by a council, and although its chief executive was
a Portreeve rather than a Mayor, Truro was ordered to send two

representatives to London to sit in the Model Parliament composed of barons, abbots, bishops, knights and representatives of the ordinary citizens. With the introduction of elected representatives, Truro kept the right to send two Members of Parliament to Westminster until the passing of Disraeli's Reform Bill in 1867.

It is beyond doubt that Truro's influence and prosperity were linked to its development and growth as a coinage town associated with the all-important minerals industry. When John Leland visited Truro at some time between 1534-43, in his capacity of 'King's Antiquary' to King Henry VIII, he reported: 'Truro is a Borow Toun and privilegid with a coynage of tynne at Midsomer and Michelmas.

'There is a Castelle a Quarter of a Mile by West out of Truro longging to the Earle of Cornwall now clene doune. The site thereof is now usid for a shoting and playing Place.'

In 1584, John Norden called at Truro as he worked on his massive task of creating the first-ever maps of Britain to record roads and distances with complete accuracy. He wrote: 'In the Cornish language they call it Trusco, seated betwene two rivers. It is an incorporation governed by a Mayre as chiefe officer and is the place of all generall assemblyes for the South and Weste divisions of the Shyre.'

The General Sessions of the Justices were held 'on frydaye and saturdaye' and Truro, he found, was one of the 'Borow-tounes' entitled, by permission of the Duke of Cornwall, 'to send Burgesses to the Parliamente.'

If the date of Norden's visit — 1584 — is correct, then Truro had rather jumped the gun, for the various rights, dignities and privileges of which he wrote were not, in fact, restated until the Charter of 1589 granted by Queen Elizabeth I, which permitted Truro 'freedom from toll, and power to hold an assize of bread and wine and to hold fairs which shall have courts of hoof-powder or toulfery, together with all liberties and free customs to such courts belonging.'

Truro was central to west Cornwall and had access to the sea through Falmouth harbour. Its industries were therefore those of the sea and the coast as much as of the land and these were recognised in its Coat-of-Arms. During the Herald's Visitation of Cornwall, these were confirmed, on 9 October 1620 (and for a fee of £3.6s — £3.30) as being: Arms — On a base barry wavy of four, charged with two fish, a three-masted ship in full sail. Also two Seals. One representing a vessel with one mast sailing, one fish in the sea, and

Inscribed *Sigilium Communitatis De Truro*. The other, a one-masted vessel with no sail, two fishes in pale in the sea, and Inscribed *Sigillum Commune Trururie*.

At this time, there were only eleven major towns in Cornwall, and of these only Truro and Launceston had the right both to Arms and Common Seals, and Truro alone was accorded the right to describe itself as 'Ancient'.

Truro's motto, *Exaltatum Cornu In Deo*, was suggested by the City's first Bishop. Although it was based on the words of Hannah's song, as recorded in the book of Samuel — 'Mine horn is exalted in the Lord' — it was a clever pun that suggested 'Cornu' for Cornwall through the historic name of Cornubia, and also suggested the horn-shape of Cornwall. As the Bishop put it: 'It is graceful for Truro to wish to share her honour with all Cornwall (on her designation as a City), as if she felt that all Cornwall would rejoice with her.'

The Civil War divided Cornwall as deeply and lastingly as any other county. Truro could not avoid involvement in the clash between Crown and Parliament and entered the conflict as a garrison town for no less than nine brigades of Royalist troops as they were driven westwards by the onslaught of the well-trained, and perhaps more dedicated, soldiers of Cromwell commanded by Sir Thomas Fairfax.

While Pendennis Castle, Falmouth, gallantly underwent a long siege and eventually surrendered to 'the most honourable terms' ever accorded by Fairfax to the vanquished, Truro was clearly a town that was not designed to withstand a long and total isolation from stores and the outside world. In 1646, the Royalist commander, Sir Ralph Hopton, surrendered his army and the town to Fairfax, and Truro had the double ignominy of not only quartering the Parliamentary troops of occupation, but of also being used as a prison for captured Royalists.

Although the rest of Cornwall eventually understood Truro's unwilling role in the latter years of the Civil War, it was many decades before understanding gave way to acceptance and, ultimately, to forgiveness and re-acceptance.

The re-emergence of the Monarchy led to a restoration of some of Truro's importance and duties. The Stannary Court, dealing with the interests and problems of the mines and miners, continued to meet until, in 1752, the Stannary Parliament met there for the last time. From then onwards, Truro enjoyed the life of a typical Cornish market town. It had its share of bull-baiting, bear-baiting, and cock-fighting. Occasionally church services, irrespective of denomination, were interrupted by dissenters. The private papers of one young citizen tell of his being advised to take a pocketful of stones 'when Mr. Wesley passes by'.

There was, too, the strange custom of 'Singing Funerals'. Whereas, in other Cornish towns, funerals were observed in something approaching total silence, they were often — in Truro — occasions for processional hymn-singing and the music of brass bands. On one occasion, in 1858, the singing of the mourners at the burial of a former publican created such a disturbance that even the tolerance of a normally moderate minister was offended by the vociferous fervour of the former customers.

Looking out over Boscawen Street for much of the City's modern history was the beautiful and imposing Red Lion hotel. In common with many of the better features of life, it has now given way to a supermarket. But even in absence, it is still revered, renowned and remembered by all true Truronians. For many people the Red Lion was as much Truro as the market, the City Hall, or even the cathedral itself.

Although, to some, it appeared ageless, it probably had its roots way back in the sixteenth century, and became a building of charm and atmosphere with its Tudor-style frontage, its covered courtyard, its Jacobean staircase, and its massive dining room. For several centuries it was the pivot of local affairs and the meeting place of scholars, businessmen and all those with a love of Truro flowing proudly through their veins.

From 1671 it housed the Foote family but, in 1769, Mr Edward Giddy proudly announced: 'In future the House called Mr. Foote's Great House will be used as the Red Lion Inn and Tavern . . . it will become by far the compleatest in Cornwall for an Inn and Tavern; and there is the most promising opening for an expert landlord to make a fortune.'

The purchaser turned out to be a Mr Thomas Gatty, who had owned the very dilapidated Old Red Lyon inn. He opened the former Foote home as 'by far the best in Cornwall', and promised: 'all who are pleased to favour me may depend on meeting with the most agreeable accommodations as I shall take care to have exceeding good beds and stabling, and to lay in the best provisions and wines of every kind.'

He kept his word and for almost two hundred years Gatty's policy

8

was neither disregarded nor discarded. It is a tribute to him, and his successors, that whilst countless thousands of visitors come to Cornwall and look at the cathedral, thousands of Cornishmen think with love and affection of the Red Lion.

They admire a cathedral . . . but the warmth of memory is for a hotel!

KEEPING THE PEACE

The fact that it now houses one of the most impressive police stations in Devon and Cornwall, and once provided accommodation for two separate police forces might seem to suggest that Truro is an oasis of crime set in rural tranquillity. In fact the reverse is true, and the City has a record no worse than any other Cornish community.

Until the early 1830s, Truro's law enforcement was the duty of a system of parish watchmen. However, in 1838, the town council decided to appoint a full-time force consisting of an Inspector and five Constables, each to wear a distinctive uniform, and to be paid at the rate of £1.10s (£1.50) per week for the Inspector, and 13s (65p) for the Constables. Looking towards the examples and standards of the Metropolitan police, Truro appointed a former London police officer to the post of Inspector and, from a list of sixteen applicants, made the remaining selection. Under the influence of the Inspector, a Mr Paine, the town council decided to dress their men in uniforms very similar to those of London, in 'blue coat and trowsers, hat, great coat and cape, lantern and staff, rattle and handcuffs, each officer to wear on his collar the town arms and his number'. Although there was a strong feeling that the force was too small to supervise a town of eleven thousand people, the Truro Constabulary soon established a close bond with the inhabitants.

Competition for membership was keen, and when an advertisement was published in 1841 for 'Parties desirous of filling the situation of a Policeman . . . testimonials as to fitness and character should be brought to the Council at the same time by Competitors who must be within the ages of 25 and 40 years', there was a queue of would-be lawmen.

With the creation of Cornwall County Constabulary in 1857, Truro occupied a dual role. It became the district headquarters for the County force who, in the main, looked after the rural areas, but continued to be served by the borough force for domestic matters, including sanitary inspections, health regulations, and weights and measures enforcement.

By 1905, the Truro police had grown both in size and in scope and consisted of a Chief Constable, two Sergeants, and nine Constables, operating from a police station and borough gaol attached to the Town Hall and Market House, in Boscawen Street, while the enlarged County Constabulary were based in their own district police station at the foot of St Clement's Hill.

In 1909, obviously alarmed by the growth of the numbers of motor vehicles on the road, the Truro Chief Constable recommended a speed limit of ten miles per hour. Clearly feeling that the motor car would never become widely owned, he recommended — in 1911 — the purchase of a bicycle to increase the mobility of his own force!

Truro could boast that its own police were motivated by spirit rather than by personal gain, for in 1919, it had the lowest paid force in Britain, a Constable earning a maximum of £2 per week and a Sergeant, for added responsibility and extra hours, being pegged to a princely £2.13s (£2.65) for a sixty-hour week.

This led to a growing friction between the 'locals' and the County men and, in 1919, the Home Office suggested the amalgamation of the Truro City Police with Cornwall County Constabulary. In March 1921, the City badges disappeared from serge collars to be replaced by the County badge.

All functions were transferred to the County police station which remained, virtually unchanged until, in 1974, it was — in turn — demolished to make way for a district and sub-divisional headquarters for the Devon and Cornwall Constabulary created by a further series of amalgamations in the mid-1960s.

Crime in Truro has always tended to be social, or even colourful, rather than seriously criminal. In 1816, for instance, two men were sentenced to be imprisoned for six months and then to be publicly flogged through the streets of Truro. Their crime? They stole a number of plants, including a rhododendron.

In 1818, John Harry was declared to be a transvestite felon, possessing a 'squeaking effeminate voice, an insinuating, or rather canting hypocritical manner of expression; addressing himself with great assiduity to the person with whom he converses; and by a kind of whining familiarity, peculiarly his own, deceives, and imposes upon every one, with whom he gains the least footing of friendship'. A reward of ten guineas was offered for his arrest.

Then there were offences of short measure. A series of raids on

Truro market, in 1828, unearthed all sorts of trickery against customers. Butter, it seems, was the target. Packages containing a professed total of 15 lbs were seized by the Constables as being underweight, and were given to the poor. The police detected one particularly clever piece of deception operated by a saleswoman. As she passed each pat of butter to be weighed, she stuck on a small extra piece weighing a couple of ounces. As the butter, after weighing, was handed back for wrapping, she was seen to remove the extra item which, when weighed, was found to be of about two ounces. She was thus weighing eight ounces, charging for eight ounces, but actually only handing six ounces to the customer.

Truro, too, suffered from the vandalism, hooliganism and high spirits associated with too much beer at too low a price. Although a copper kettle used as a sign over the doorway of a shop was recovered next morning from the top of a lamp, traders were warned — in 1833 — never to expose valuable signs or other articles to public temptation.

The year 1848 brought a new dimension to crime — the theft of bees and hives — and the warning that the next year's honey crop could be in danger from the activities of thieves. Dealers were warned that as the 'honest' season had passed, anyone offering bees, hives or honey must be suspected of being dishonest.

Although Truro took crime in its stride, it developed a strong social conscience in the matter of punishment.

In 1848, the then Mayor was publicly criticised for his action in punishing a young woman named Murton. A year earlier, having been fined for disorderly behaviour, she fled town rather than pay the fine. Twelve months later she foolishly returned, was arrested, and taken before the Mayor. He ordered her to be placed in the stocks for six hours. This, *The West Briton* found, 'was a most brutal and indecent punishment'. Fortunately a local resident was so outraged that, together with some friends, he immediately paid the fine and secured the girl's release.

The newspaper, however, mounted an unprecedented attack on the town's first citizen: 'We have been so much accustomed to the strange proceedings of the Mayor of Truro, that nothing which he does can now surprise us, and any remark upon his conduct in the present case is almost uncalled for. We may state however, that the law on which he professed to act, dates back so far as the reign of James the First, and in so far as the punishment of the stocks is concerned, is generally, we believe, regarded as obsolete. In all probability there is not another magistrate in England who upon such authority would, in the case of a woman at least, have revived a punishment so out of date, and so utterly opposed to the spirit and feelings of the present day.'

The stocks were not used again and the Mayor was not re-elected which was, perhaps, fortunate for Grace Stephens who ran a brothel in Calenick Street in 1849, and who received six months in prison for her activities in organising a band of prostitutes authoritatively described by a neighbour, Mr Crowle, as being 'as bad as the worst I would expect to meet with in the worst parts of England'. Was Mr Crowle speaking from experience or from hearsay? History is as elusive on that point as on the identity of the savage Mayor.

There will be those who argue that a severity of punishment kept crime in check, while others will claim that there is nothing more effective than a truly local police force constantly drawing from its personal knowledge of would-be offenders.

Whatever the reason, a glance at the crime figures for 1868 would seem to suggest that Truro had no problems of any magnitude. In that year, out of a population of over eleven thousand people, only thirteen men and six women were charged with serious offences. In the field of minor crime, one hundred and forty one men and nine women were convicted, thirty four going to prison, four whipped, and four remanded to await Army or Naval escorts. Disorderly conduct, drink, prostitution, vagrancy and petty theft were the most common causes of an appearance before the local magistrates.

The borough lock-up was, admittedly, no home from home. It had no toilet facilities, no ventilation, and little privacy. The floor of each of the three communal cells was covered in straw and in the centre of each room was a solid wooden block to which violent prisoners or possible escapees could be chained. Magistrates had, therefore, to decide on the most appropriate form of punishment since nobody could be imprisoned there for long and had either to be sent to the County prison at Bodmin, at great public cost and inconvenience, or else allowed to go home after being fined or at least detained for a few days. Thus it was that female offenders were often shorn of their hair to provide a moderately permanent reminder of their conviction.

Less fortunate were offenders against Army or Naval discipline, particularly those arrested for desertion. In 1831, a deserter was sentenced to five hundred lashes at Truro barracks. Although he fainted three times and was revived, the sentence was only abandoned half-way through the ordeal. Another man was 'saved' from the final one hundred lashes of a four-hundred-lash sentence imposed for leaving barracks, out of hours, to go across the road for a glass of beer.

Despite the furore over the woman, Murton, in the stocks in 1848, some offenders regarded this form of punishment with absolute contempt. In 1844, one woman was recorded as having spent the time perched on a 'pillow' of straw and knitting as comfortably and unconcernedly as if she had been in the living room at home. Her fellow prisoner at least had the decency (or perhaps the diplomatic wisdom) to be seen to weep and show signs of distress and atonement for her crime of drunkenness.

But it was not always the police or magistrate who dispensed retribution. Sometimes there was an aura of poetic justice as well. When an intruder entered a potato warehouse on Lemon Quay, on a January night in 1851, he had no reason to suspect that his constant filching of a few potatoes at a time over several months had been noticed, especially as they had been removed from the back of a pile through a hole in the weatherboarding of a wall. As he pushed his hand through the crack, there was a flash of metal; teeth whirred through the air; man-made spring-loaded jaws sprang shut. Although stealing was illegal, the use of the gin-trap was not. Held by the fingers as securely as by police handcuffs on the wrists, the young man's agony was only relieved by the arrival of the potato merchant.

14

PRIVIES,
PRESCRIPTIONS AND PIGS

Two massive hospitals — the City, and the Royal Cornwall (Treliske) — could cause the uncharitable to say that Truro does very well out of illness or, even less charitably, that it has a massive preoccupation with the physical weaknesses of the flesh.

Neither, however, is even remotely true. The two hospitals serve Cornwall as a whole rather than merely Truro as a City, and if there is an apparent preoccupation with its own health, then Truro has had the type of history of poor health that justifies its caution.

Disease has been no stranger to Truro. In fact the Black Death might well have helped establish the settlement that grew into today's City, for it was in 1410, following an outbreak of the disease, that local folk petitioned Parliament for permission to levy a special sum to stem the exodus of those fleeing Truro on the approach of the plague and to restore the houses abandoned by those who had fled.

Cholera and rabies, too, were to play their part in the growth of a riverside town with its problems of drainage and flooding. In the case of rabies, the stores, warehouses and ships associated with port activities attracted rats. The rats, in turn, drew packs of dogs. In almost every Cornish town but Truro, local councils hurriedly passed regulations on the control of dogs insisting that they be muzzled by day and face the probability of extermination if found unmuzzled. Under pressure, Truro became the last town to conform, in 1824.

But it was cholera that was to be the biggest and most repeated threat, striking Truro in 1832, 1833, 1849, 1853 and 1866, with smallpox intervening in 1865.

In 1832, the Truro Port Health Authority acted with all the wisdom of King Canute in refusing permission for the body of a seaman who had died from cholera to be brought ashore. Either way they could not win. Whether it was buried ashore or isolated on the ship at its quarantine anchorage, the body posed the threat of infection.

Truro provided an ideal setting for the growth and spread of disease. A combination of courtyards, alleys and narrow streets created so bewildering a pattern of houses and accesses that the droppings of horses, humans, dogs and cattle could lie, unattended, for long periods. The Commissioners of Paving and Lighting did their best, but their best was limited both by manpower and other resources.

They made a start, in 1833, by clearing the Kenwyn River and the various common drains leading into it. But the river merely became an open sewer. The Commissioners loaned brushes and buckets to anyone too poor to have even the most primitive forms of sanitation. But as the contents of the buckets were emptied into the streams and waterways, the risk of infection grew.

Twenty years later, in 1853, it was discovered that the new measures were to little effect. Even in the prime residential area of Lemon Street, it was discovered that 'backlets' were in so disgusting a state of filth that they could not be equalled elsewhere in Truro. The Commissioners found that many 'respectable' houses had just not been connected to main sewers, and that toilets had not been cleaned out for years at a time. 'We believe it would be advisable that no house whatever should be exempted from a visitation in order to enforce attention to sanitary regulations,' the report recommended. 'The want of attention to cleanliness is by no means exclusively confined to the lower class of inhabitants.'

By 1859 the authorities were in danger of over-reacting. A ban was placed on the passage of human waste and household refuse through the streets in daytime. Consequently rubbish and human excrement would be allowed to amass in the house until last thing at night when it could be taken to a disposal point. In bad weather, or in the case of the sick or the elderly, it was not always possible to remove the matter during the appointed hours, so it could sometimes remain in the house for two or three days at a time, all the time the occupants inhaling the stench and running the risk of infection.

If the means of waste disposal were suspect, then water supplies were almost certain to lead to massive health problems. By 1871, with five outbreaks of cholera and one of smallpox already a matter for the records and for the files of the undertakers and sextons, the water supply for a town of eleven thousand people was limited to twenty-five public pumps, two wells, and an open stream caressing the pavements but carrying with it the contents of water closets,

1 New Bridge, 1900

2   The Author

▲ 3   Truro Cathedral - southside   4   Truro Police Station ▼

5   Boscawen Street 1911

6 Red Lion Hotel 1920

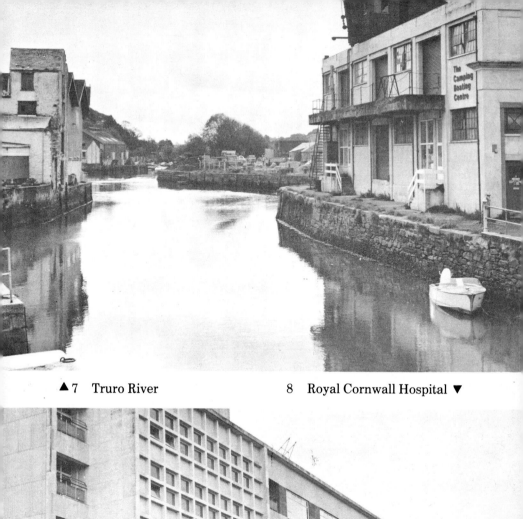

▲ 7 Truro River   8 Royal Cornwall Hospital ▼

9 Riverside Warehouse

10 Bowling Green 1939

11   Bowling Green 1978

12   Lemon Quay 1910

13   Lemon Quay 1920

14 Boscawen Street 1910

15   Boscawen Street 1920

16 Boscawen Street 1930

17   Snow Scene 1891

18   Town Quay 1920

animal droppings, and the washings of the intestines of cattle. To make matters worse, one pump was in an abandoned graveyard and in constant danger of pollution.

Help was at hand in the form of a newly-appointed Surveyor, William Clemens. He ordered an immediate assault on what he suspected to be the causes of disease. He organised the sluice gates on Truro's rivers so that when they were opened twice daily, cascading an estimated half a million gallons of water before them, the effect would be to swill refuse and sewage into the tidal waters downstream.

Next he turned his attention to other aspects of public health. Under a new bye-law, it became an offence to keep a pig within thirty yards of a dwelling house. Although one hundred and seventy porkers became homeless, the centre of Truro became a pig-free zone, with an immediate and obvious improvement in both sound and smell.

From pigs to pipes. Up came the old stone sewers, and in went two miles of pipe drains. He ordered the closing of one hundred and forty seven cesspits, and supervised the provision of one hundred and fifty five soil-pans and water closets.

Health and hygiene had arrived, thanks to William Clemens. Unfortunately the public was not in any obvious haste to take advantage of the new facilities. Indeed, at the time of a typhoid outbreak in 1878, even the Royal Cornwall Infirmary was not connected to the public sewer which ran but a few yards away.

Clemens encountered another problem. Although he could assess the number of houses there were in Truro needing connection to water and drainage, and although he had a rough idea of the overall size of the population, he could not get accurate details of the number of occupants per household. The Council Improvement Committee researched the problem and came up with horrifying figures of overcrowding. In just one room of one house they found two adults and five children; in another, three adults and ten children occupying one living room and four bedrooms in a shared house. In yet another house, four adults and four children using but two bedrooms. Another roof housed, in two tiny bedrooms, four adults and six children; while a different address provided a bedroom occupied by a husband and wife and their five youngsters.

Although the figures are bad enough, the fact that they are as recent as 1892 would seem to suggest the unwillingness of Truro people, even then, to accept that disease was a curse that was being self-generated by their own unwillingness to take advantage of the social, health and welfare services being provided for them. Disease, it seemed, was almost accepted as an inevitability of nineteenth century life.

If there was scant attention to life, there was an overwhelming preoccupation with death, and Truro must be one of the few towns in Britain that has regularly included its cemeteries in its list of attractions. A guide to Truro published in 1883 mentions a general cemetery situated on St Clement's Hill, established in 1840. With a delightful piece of unwitting humour it refers to the management being in the hands of 'a body' of shareholders! The description is of a burial ground 'badly kept and requiring enlargement'. Clearly the bad state of upkeep might have been due to insufficient revenue for, the guide says, 'There are no fixed fees for ministers, but it is expected that friends will always remember a voluntary offering.' Either there were few friends, or memories were both short and minimal.

By 1905, however, Truro was boasting of its new cemetery with the same pride that Newquay was advertising its newest hotels: 'The new general cemetery is situated on St. Clement's-hill, directly opposite the old Cemetery Company's ground. It commands very extensive views of the surrounding country. Truro now possesses the best arranged and most pleasantly situated cemetery in the County.'

Despite the undoubted environmental satisfaction of the dead, Truro has an even longer — and far more proud — record of activity in the field of surgery and medicine. The Royal Cornwall Infirmary, now known as The Royal Cornwall Hospital (City), dates from the late eighteenth century, and was created through the generosity of the three great Cornish families of the day, the Bassets, the Lemons and the St Aubyns, although an inscribed tablet merely refers to 'the establishment, permanency and usefulness of the charity to be chiefly due to the munificent liberality and unwearied exertions of Francis Lord de Dunstanville'.

What is interesting in the history of this great hospital is that, until 1906, it was used exclusively for the poor on a non-payment basis and that the wealthy were expected to go elsewhere for treatment. It was gradually recognised that since the well-off were among the main supporters, it was unreasonable to exclude them. So, in 1906, the first fee-paying patients were admitted, and by 1920, every patient was expected to pay a small sum towards their costs. This continued until the Royal Cornwall Infirmary was taken into the National Health Service in 1946, and the emphasis on free treatment was reinstated.

Twenty years later the new Royal Cornwall Hospital (Treliske) was opened on the outskirts of Truro to provide a health service facility second to none.

If the introduction of the National Health Service meant a new role for the Royal Cornwall Infirmary, it sounded the death knell for another Truro institution, the Truro Dispensary, which had been set up in 1842 'to afford advice and medicine to necessitous persons, on their application at the dispensary with a ticket of recommendation from a subscriber'.

The Dispensary was under the control of the Mayor, a banker, a solicitor, a physician and surgeon and twelve other subscribers. In return for their subscriptions, these gentlemen were each allocated an agreed number of 'tickets of recommendation', each guaranteeing six weeks of free treatment to a poor person, to be distributed at their discretion. Unlike similar schemes in other towns, the Truro Dispensary was unique in that, wherever and whenever necessary, the doctors carried out home visits as well as their normal consultations in the Dispensary.

With the close-knit and terraced nature of housing in Truro, fire was a constant threat, the danger being enlarged both by the high proportion of thatched dwellings and by the large number of fire-risk industries, such as kilns, wool warehouses and bakeries. Yet it was not until the formation of the Volunteer Fire Brigade, in 1868, with its thirty men and two appliances, that a permanent fire-fighting team came into being.

Quartered in St Mary's Street, it had to resort to raffles, bazaars and fêtes to keep itself clad, mobile and equipped. Although the insurance companies paid large contributions, the brigade had to be largely self-supporting.

In 1904 the fire station was moved to the rear of the Town Hall, and the brigade was able to announce to a reassured public that it had grown to consist of: 'A Captain, a First Lieutenant, a Second Lieutenant, three Superintendents, a Superintendent of fire escape, an engineer and ten firemen. Three excellent engines and all necessary appliances are kept in perfect order, ready at a moment's notice, night or day. In all cases of fire, notice must first be given at the Borough Police Station, when the Brigade will be immediately summoned by the Police, the station having electric communication with each fireman.'

Electricity was, by 1904, no new-fangled innovation for Truro, and had been gradually introduced — in various forms — from 1890 onwards. Until the mid-1800s, there had been complaints about the inadequacy of street lighting supplied by the Truro Gas Company at the request of the Commissioners of Paving and Lighting. It was switched on too late, switched off too early, and of dubious quality, it was claimed. In fact, it was generalised, the only people who gained any benefit were the criminal fraternity.

This was grossly untrue and unfair, since from 1810 Truro had possessed its own gas works and had become one of Britain's first towns to have its own source of supply and to embark on a massive scheme of public lighting. Indeed, were the service not reliable, the City would not have delayed the changeover to electricity for its street lights until the late 1930s.

If ever the Gas or Electricity companies were to do battle as to the most effective way of cooking mutton, the chances are that Truro folk would have already decided that particular issue! In 1819, they were given the chance of seeing the Russian fire-proof phenomena, Monsieur and Mademoiselle Chabert repeat their party-piece (for a fee of not less than £500) of entering an oven with a joint of mutton and staying with it until it was cooked. Truro's scepticism for a 'Russian' couple with a French name was such that the £500 was not forthcoming, and the audience in the Assembly Rooms had to make do with more down-to-earth parlour tricks such as eating lighted candles; chewing melted sealing wax; and holding molten lead and boiling oil in the mouth.

For music lovers there were the occasional visits of Richardson's Rock Band and Chinese Steel Band in the 1840s, seemingly giving 'the highest pleasure' to those who appreciated sacred and classical music played on pieces of rock or on steel plates struck with mallets 'with exquisite taste and feeling'.

A far more callous pursuit was to release as many as thirty rabbits held captive in a box, to see how many could be killed or maimed by a group of men with guns before the unfortunate creatures reached the safety of the hedges of Kenwyn.

But, ever full of mystery, wonder, challenge, spectacle and delight, were the Truro Whitsun Fairs. In 1811, the attractions included

36

the diminutive 54-year old 'Windsor Fairy' who, it was claimed, had so delighted King George III that he created her the Lady Morgan, in recognition of the fine display of human nature contained in her tiny frame. Then, in 1845, came Wombwell's Menagerie, 'an excellent collection in which the proprietor has invested a princely capital, beyond all praise, and worth seeing at any time'.

By 1861 the railway was carrying trippers to the Truro Fair. In one day more than two thousand people travelled by rail from Falmouth, Redruth, Camborne and Penzance alone to see such shows as Quaglieni's Royal Sardinian Circus, Mander's Menagerie, and Weight's Theatre, all agreeing with the verdict of the local Press that the offerings added up to more attractions and novelties than had been seen at Truro for many years.

For those of more unusual taste, there was the spectacle of the man who, 'for a trifling wager' would eat two live eels, bones and all. But there was a disappointment for the fans of a certain Frenchman. According to his reputation, his speciality was to have a meal of live rats. He may have got away with it at Redruth and St Austell, but Truro decided to take a stand. On the night before the Whitsun Fair of 1864 was due to open, Superintendent Woolcock, of the local police, served notice that Truro, at least, would not tolerate the eating of rats, whether dead or alive.

The point was taken and dozens of disappointed fans had to content themselves with seeing their hero slobber his bloody way through seemingly endless plates of raw liver.

SCHOONERS,
SMUGGLERS AND SILT

With the self-important clatter and bustle of the local dredger fighting a tireless battle against mudbanks and silt, it seems almost impossible to accept that Truro was once one of Cornwall's most important ports.

Worth's Quay, Lemon Quay, Enys Quay, Town Quay, Quay Street and Duchy Wharf, all point to a maritime association far more intimate and important even than the three-masted ship in full sail so prominently featured in the Arms of the City.

As far back as the year 1160, Truro was exporting wool and tin, and importing wine and dried fish. Its prosperity acted as a magnet to raiders and, in 1377 and 1404, it was attacked by the French. On the first occasion warehouses were looted and ships taken away; and on the second there was a major attempt to burn the township to the ground. Truro survived and, by the late 1400s, had become a major centre of commercial shipping due to the convenience of its position to the growing demands of the mining industry.

The Port of Truro once extended to cover the whole of Falmouth harbour, and it was claimed that 'the Mayor of Truro hath always been, and still is, Mayor of Falmouth, as by ancient grant now in the custody of the said Mayor and Burgesses doth appear'. This statement was a rather liberal interpretation of a charter granted by King John, and restated by Queen Elizabeth in 1589.

Falmouth disputed this, but Truro continued to claim jurisdiction of all waters from the head of the Truro river to the entrance to Falmouth harbour. It was not merely a matter of local pride. The two rival townships had been at loggerheads for many years. In 1613, Truro — together with Penryn and Helston — had objected to the plans of Sir John Killigrew to develop a town and port at what was to become Falmouth.

In the Civil War, Truro surrendered to the Parliamentary forces of General Fairfax. Falmouth, on the other hand, remained loyal and it was through that town that Prince Charles made his escape. When the monarchy was restored, one of his first acts was to grant Falmouth a charter in 1661. So that nobody could doubt that this was a deliberate snub to Truro, the new king gave Falmouth rights over the harbour as well. The effects on Truro's trade were both immediate and severe and, by 1695, it had become 'a ruinated disregarded place'.

The older town re-asserted its rights. Falmouth resisted and took Truro to Court. The result was not exactly pleasing to the upriver port. Falmouth was recognised as being of more importance than the river-head town nine miles away. In 1709 the Courts ruled that, in future, the Port of Truro should run only as far as a line drawn across Carrick Roads from Messack, near St Just-in-Roseland, to Mylor.

From 1709 until the reorganisation of Local Government in 1974, Truro took regular and elaborate steps to restate its claim on such of its port as it had been allowed to retain. Every sixth year the council carried out the serious duty of 'Renewing the Water Bounds of the Port and Harbour of Truro', including the strange custom of the 'arrest-for-debt' of a totally honourable, honest and debt-free citizen!

In solemn procession, the dignitaries went aboard boats at Lemon Quay and made the journey to the outer limits of their jurisdiction, 'to renew the rights liberties and precincts of the City and Port of Truro', and to symbolically recut the letters 'T.B.' in the granite stones on the shoreline marking the limits. The harbourmaster, in his role of Water Bailiff of the City, his authority represented by his Silver Oar, then formally arrested one of the party for an undisclosed indebtedness of £999.19.11¾d, immediately releasing the debtor to two other prominent citizens in response to sureties of £500 apiece. Presumably, in this way, the Water Bailiff could always be certain of a working profit of at least one farthing at the end of each six year cycle.

Even more serious was the 'discovery' at each point that the 'F.B.' (Falmouth Borough) stones had invaded Truro's territory. The Mayor was instructed to report this to the next meeting of the council. Then, with the loud voice of the town crier announcing that the Water Bounds had been renewed, the Truro party would withdraw upstream for another six years.

Even had Falmouth not won the day, in 1709, Truro's continuation as a major port would have been in grave doubt. Better roads and larger ships would eventually have reduced its importance and its accessibility. Gradually its merchants became shipping agents rather than shipowners, and the ships that negotiated the beautiful river became those of the coastal rather than the deep-sea trade.

But somehow it held on to its maritime links for another two hundred and fifty years, much of it in the form of cargo transhipped at Falmouth. Fleets of barges worked their way up and down river with coal, tin-ore, fertiliser, lime, and the impedimenta of growing industrialisation. Competition was keen. The hours were long, the task heavy. To make even a decent living, the bargees had to load and unload swiftly since there was no money to be earned by an idle vessel.

The quays were still a scene of great activity, with horses drawing huge low wagons of mine supplies up the steep hills around the town, or threatening to be run down by runaway trucks on the approaches to the riverside.

In the 1820s there were still upwards of thirty sea-going vessels, mostly schooners, operating out of Truro to Russia, France, the Mediterranean, to London and to South Wales. In one week, in January 1822, there were five arrivals from the coal ports of South Wales, and one from Plymouth, as well as ten ships sailing for Wales and one for Liverpool. Fifty years later, trade was as brisk. In the ten days from 17 March to 26 March 1873, forty-two ships arrived with coal, nitrates, timber, grain and flour.

Not all arrivals were registered with the authorities, for the Truro River had an undoubted appeal for the smuggling fraternity. In 1837, the brig *Mercury* was intercepted by the Excisemen. She was carrying one hundred and thirty tons of brandy. According to the normal procedure, she was taken to Truro, broken-up, and sold as a miscellany of spare parts.

The same fate befell another vessel, this time a schooner, spotted by Preventive Officers in Truro Port waters. As the revenue cutter gave chase, the suspect — identified as a former Packet ship — headed for the shore. The crew jumped onto the river bank and disappeared into the surrounding countryside leaving a vast haul of brandy and other spirits behind.

Truro's loss of status as a port was gradual . . . so gradual, in fact, that perhaps few Truronians were actually aware of it. When the council decided, in 1888, to improve the pavements alongside the wharves of Lemon Quay nobody could have guessed that within but a further few decades, the whole area would have become a massive car park and that maritime activities would have been relegated to the golden memories of older generations.

Perhaps, in 1888, there was a warning. Announcing the scheme for a better pavement, *The West Briton* reported that 'none but our older readers' would recall when the area resounded to the sounds of the shipwright's craft and, amid the heady aroma of best pine, oak, and the purest tar and pitch, a proud line of Truro-built ketches and sloops were laid down, launched and completed. These were the merchant schooners that were to carry Truro's craftsmanship to Newfoundland and Brazil, and around the ports of Europe, built in the yards of Charles Dyer, Peter and William Ferris, Nicholas Scoble, and the Stephens family.

Among the most popular ships operating out of Truro was John Stephens' *Henrietta*, which ran between Devoran and London with general cargo from 1872. Later she was sold to a Newquay owner, and was lost after a collision in the Mersey while sailing to Liverpool.

Another familiar sight alongside Lemon Quay was the Ipswich-built brigantine, *Flora*, which ran to London via the Channel Islands with general cargo, or to Corunna to bring back cattle for unloading at Penryn. There was a great feeling of personal loss in Truro when, in 1883, *Flora* was lost on Hasboro Sands.

Right up to the 1960s and the early 1970s, Truro kept its sea trade open with shipments of coal and, occasionally, of timber, but now the quays are virtually silent except for the excited chatter of trippers setting off on one of Cornwall's most beautiful river journeys, past Malpas and King Harry Ferry, and through Carrick Roads to Falmouth.

ROADS, COACHES AND TRAINS

Although the book — the prayer book or the school book — has been influential in the development of Truro, it is the wheel that has played an even more important role over a much longer period.

It just isn't possible to find a map of Cornwall without Truro appearing on it. All roads, it seems, lead there or else pass so close as to make no difference.

The erratic wheels of carts and wagons; the precision wheels of mail-coaches; the pneumatic wheels of lorries and buses; the flanged wheels of railway trucks and coaches; the wheels that have controlled the sluice gates on the rivers; all these have been vital to Truro's prosperity and success.

Roads, too, have always been given loving care. In 1822, for instance, it was decided that the state of the turnpike roads serving Truro would be made safer and more comfortable by the use of small stones rather than large ones. Although the new method was both tedious and costly, the benefits were lasting.

But the romance of Truro's roads was the romance of use rather than of construction. In 1829, road users and pedestrians were asked to adopt a local highway code whereby walkers would move to the right when confronted by folk going in the other direction on the narrow pavements. The Mayor also requested citizens not to assemble in groups on street corners, to thus keep the way clear of interruption and obstruction for respectable females.

The year 1838 brought a new menace — small boys playing with hoops in the main thoroughfares. Law officers were instructed to confiscate 'these objects which cause, alike, inconvenience and danger to persons walking, but more particularly to persons riding or driving'.

Speeding offences became commonplace, and on one day in 1844, the local Magistrate found that no less than sixteen van owners had permitted their drivers to proceed at a speed in excess of four miles per hour. The fines ranged from £5 to £20, with imprisonment of from one to three months if the fines were not paid within fourteen days.

By 1869, maximum speeds had been increased, and it was regarded as perfectly proper that 'the locomotive machines known as velocipedes, and engaging the attention of machinists and engineers with these useful and powerful carriages' could be driven at up to fifteen miles per hour 'upon a fair road'.

Nine years later, however, it was the pedestrian rather than the driver who was back in trouble. Once more it was a question of walkers not obeying the rules of the pavement, and the City Council was asked to consider exhibiting notices at the corners of all main streets instructing those on foot to keep to the right, especially on 'market-days, or on other occasions when there are more people about than usual'.

Realising that the arrival of the railway would increase both the weight and frequency of heavy freight through the City, the far-sighted Surveyor, Mr Clemens, carried out a massive scheme of resurfacing central roads in the 1880s, and when the motor car pioneer, Mr Henry Sturmey, drove his five-seater car through Truro in 1897 on the first journey by automobile from John O'Groats to Land's End, he was able to report that Cornwall's roads were better than any in France, Germany, Belgium or Holland, and certainly the best in the United Kingdom.

Truro had been a main town on the coaching network from the early 1700s, although its services dated back even further than that. In 1759 there were scheduled routes to Exeter and beyond, as well as to Falmouth, Grampound, Bodmin and Launceston. Within a further half century, services had been expanded to include Penzance, St Austell and Torpoint. However, a combination of overloading and bad roads led to numerous mishaps. Wheels fell off, brakes failed, and there were always the unpredictable hazards associated with a drunken coachman well fortified with spirits against the elements.

One group of travellers, in 1816, suffered the unique but terrifying experience of sitting inside the mail coach as a lion — which had escaped from a travelling circus — attacked one of the horses. The lion was recaptured and the horse, when its wounds healed, continued its career on the roads for many years.

On great occasions the Truro coaches were the focal-point of celebration. News of the short-lived Peace with France in 1814, after twenty years of warfare, arrived in Truro to the explosion of fireworks, and in a coach decorated with laurel.

When the Defiance Company beat the rival Regulator Company in establishing links from Truro to London, Birmingham and Bristol, 'a large party of gentlemen sat down to an excellent dinner', *The West Briton* recorded in 1835, 'to express a deep interest in support of the Defiance, and a strong determination to exert themselves to secure its success'.

The severe winter of 1855 led to one coach travelling from Truro to Falmouth arriving almost three hours late. Three times the horses fell on the slippery roads, and the coachman, one passenger and one horse were injured.

From then onwards, due to the growing importance of the railway, horse traffic went into a steady decline although, well into the last quarter of the nineteenth century, Truro was one of the busiest centres of the coach and wagon trade.

In 1880, a set of Hackney Carriage Regulations for vehicles registered in Truro laid down that there should be a piece of string linking the passenger to the driver 'which he must at all times hold when driving, and pay immediate attention to any signal so given'. Carriages should be driven at a rate of not less than four miles an hour. 'No driver shall use indecorous or improper language, or otherwise misbehave himself or take up any person without leave of the Hirer; and every licensed Hackney Coachman shall wear a badge, with the number of his license thereon in large figures, on his right arm, to be always visible'.

As far back as August 1847, the first steps had been taken to link Truro to the railway map of Britain. In what was described as a 'spiritless manner', the first sod was cut. Due to an acute shortage of food in the County, there were riots and demonstrations against the railway engineers and labourers, it being feared that Cornwall could not feed the extra mouths. The railway was therefore put in limbo until 1852 when shareholders were told that the Board of Trade had reduced the scope of operations and that £50 shares had been revalued to £20.

After a series of false starts and slow construction, the main line linking Truro with Plymouth was inaugurated on 4 May 1859, with the opening of the Royal Albert Bridge, at Saltash. However, a series of accidents did little to create confidence in the railway. Its critics claimed that it was actually against the interests of Cornish consumers since it caused so much local produce by way of meat,

19 Lander Monument

▲ 20   Site of Truro Grammar School   21   Truro Railway Station ▼

22   Britannia Hotel

▲ 23   Boscawen Street 1978   24   City Hall ▼

▲ 25   Walsingham Place   26   Princes House ▼

27 & 28   Victorian Pillar Boxes

29   Pydar Street 1910

30 & 31   Lemon Street

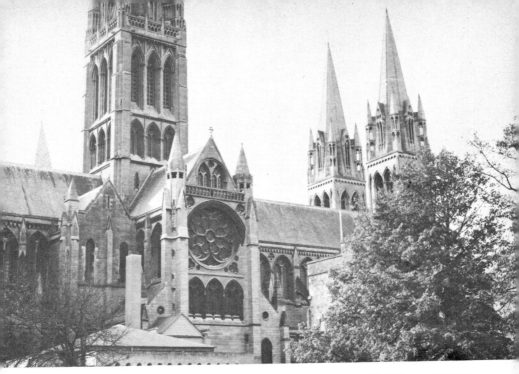

▲ 32   Truro Cathedral - north side   33   Post Office, High Cross, 1910 ▼

34 St Mary's

35　Cathedral Lane

▲ 36   Union Place   37   Pydar Street ▼

▲ 38 County Museum   39   Mansion House ▼

▲ 40 'Old' County Hall   41 'New' County Hall ▼

▲ 42   Street Scene 1920   43   Lychgate, Kenwyn ▼

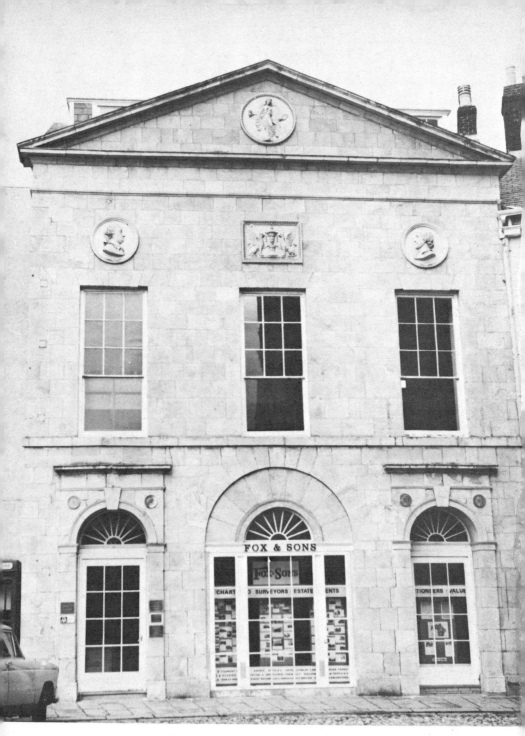

44   Assembly Rooms

fish and vegetables, to be taken to the London markets, that Cornish scarcity followed and led to artificially high food prices. By 1860, some six hundred head of sheep were passing through Truro each week, with a seasonal 'export' of one thousand tons of fish, seventeen hundred tons of potatoes and eight hundred tons of broccoli.

In the same year there were complaints about the standards of hygiene, it being alleged that third-class passengers sometimes had to travel in wagons normally used for cattle, and with traces of excrement still obviously and odorously present beside and beneath the wooden benches which had been installed for the convenience of passengers. Locks and catches, it was said, were so unreliable that — between stations — the doors flew open while, at the platform, it was easier to climb over the sides than to wrestle with the malfunctioning mechanism.

Yet, despite adverse publicity from a vociferous and influential body of protestors, the railway grew both in stature and importance. One seal of respectability was applied in 1861 when it was announced that the nationally respected firm of Pickford & Co would establish themselves in Truro to integrate their services with those of the railway operators.

Another important milestone was reached in 1866, when the final changeover from narrow gauge to broad gauge took place, and coaches and locomotives of uniform type could travel from London to Penzance. Up to that year, the Cornwall Railway from Plymouth to Truro had favoured Brunel's broad gauge of seven feet, while the West Cornwall Railway, from Truro to Penzance, was of but four feet eight and a half inches, thus requiring the offloading and reloading of all freight at Truro for West Cornwall with particular inconvenience to the consignors of perishable goods.

It was to be a costly and pointless exercise, for in 1892, the entire two hundred miles of lines through Devon and Cornwall were reduced — in an incredible four days — back to the narrow gauge that had become standard for Britain's railways. More than five thousand men worked round the clock to effect the change, and one hundred of them were accommodated in two large tents and the goods shed at Truro.

From then onwards Truro grew to a new importance for passenger and freight traffic, and the opening of branch lines to Newham and Falmouth meant fifty passenger trains a day making scheduled calls as the nineteenth century made way for the twentieth.

'THE BEST
METHODS OF EDUCATION'

At first glance, the atmosphere-laden building in St Mary's Street could be mistaken as the cradle of Truro's tradition of education. Like some tiny college outpost transplanted from a great academic university, it has the aura of learning about it. The craggy stone walls, the towered roof, the huge windows all seem to bear testimony to its scholastic tradition. Yet, in reality, it merely marks the half-way mark backwards from the education of today to the foundation of Truro Grammar School, in 1549, and indicates the site of the school rather than the buildings that housed it.

Truro's proud record as a centre of education spans more than four centuries . . . the influence of its former pupils has become worldwide in a richness of service unequalled by any other town of similar modest size and age.

Its excellence of education has been founded on an awareness of the different aspirations and abilities of parents and pupils; on religious principles, both formal and nonconformist; and on a universal target of achievement both in the 'fee-paying' and 'free' sectors of education. True, for more than two hundred years, the Truro Grammar School enjoyed a monopoly position and provided an academic springboard to the major public schools and universities.

By the early 1800s, the thirst for at least a basic education was making itself felt. It was no good looking for outstanding teachers and fine buildings if local pay packets could not meet the fees, so a less advanced form of education was introduced in 1812. Known as 'Dr Bell's System', it consisted merely of giving carefully-selected senior pupils so concentrated a course of rudimentary education that they could act as class leaders and monitors to smaller groups of youngsters studying at a basic level. As each monitor would look after, at most, two other pupils, the scheme was successful in that it could virtually guarantee the type of basic tutorial attention that would quickly encourage the basic learner to an elementary level of understanding.

62

While the fee-paying schools prospered, very real progress was made in providing a form of universal education in Truro well ahead of the requirements of the great Education Acts of 1870 and 1876. The Act of 1870 took the first faltering steps towards the free elementary education of the children of parents who could not afford to pay for it; while the Act of 1876 demanded compulsory education for children up to the age of twelve.

The six years between the two Acts were difficult ones for towns and cities with a long tradition of religious-based education. Truro was no exception. On the one hand the churches, through voluntary schools, were doing their best. Numerically, however, it was a very poor best. Truro, with a child population of over three thousand, had but one thousand school places.

Although the churches were doing all they could, their resources were not limitless. On the one hand they welcomed the setting up of School Boards to answer local educational needs; but on the other, they resented the fact that since Board Schools were undenominational, the influence of the church might be diminished. However, it was obvious that Board School places were better than no places at all. Schools were spartan and overcrowded, but at least the availability of education increased.

In 1898, a delegation of Cornish trade unionists supported a Trades-Union-Congress resolution calling for equality of opportunity in education, the provision of school meals, the abolition of the half-time system under which, in many schools, youngsters were either 'morning' or 'afternoon' pupils to offset pressure on school places, the raising of the school leaving age to fifteen, the improved training of teachers, and the transfer of all educational costs from local budgets to the National Exchequer.

Since non-fee-paying schools did not advertise for pupils, a 1905 account of the City's education is inevitably one-sided. Truro School, run on Methodist principles, claimed that, educationally, it occupied 'the first place in the County. The climate of Truro is particularly adapted for boys coming from abroad and, for many years, Truro College has had a wide connection with other countries.'

By use of 'the best methods of instruction', Truro High School could ensure, for its young ladies, 'a sound thorough education suited to their requirements.'

Truro Grammar School promised that even 'backward boys receive every care and individual attention'. In 1877 it had transferred from

St Mary's Street to Tregolls, and in 1909 — having been renamed Truro Cathedral School in 1906 — went to a spot in the Cathedral cloisters where it was to remain until a further move, in the 1960s, took it up the hill to Kenwyn.

Both Truro School and Truro High School shared the same foundation year, 1880, the High School being opened in that year by the first Bishop of Truro, Dr Benson, and Truro School some two years later by the then president of Conference, Dr Osborne. It is almost impossible to believe that Truro School, with its imposing buildings and beautiful site, was bought, built and equipped for a mere £10,000.

Also, in the category of 'fee-paying' schools was the Rosewin Training School for Servants. Inaugurated by the Association for the Care of Friendless Girls, it was run by the Sisters of the Community of the Epiphany 'for the purpose of training those girls for service who have either undesirable homes or, from some other circumstances, have not the opportunity of being properly trained'. For this opportunity they had to find £10 a year and provide their own outfit.

Truro's major educational provision was completed by the opening, in 1906, of a County Grammar School for Girls which, in 1927, moved from Strangways Terrace to larger purpose-built accommodation in Treyew Road.

Yet although Truro has traditionally provided a full choice of educational opportunity for boys and girls within the 'private' sector, for some reason it has never possessed a free grammar school for boys in the true sense of the word, although having more than answered the needs of secondary and technical education. It has taken, eventually through the arrival of the comprehensive system, perhaps far too long to provide a truly universal form of education for its boys.

INFLUENCE BEYOND THE CITY

If life could come into the sightless eyes of Richard Lander, standing forever atop his Nelson-like column and facing down Lemon Street and over the rooftops of Truro, they would immediately spot a strange fact.

Although Truro has seen the birth of many great men in the fields of art, culture, exploration and military affairs — and has provided a home to many who have inspired or encouraged the lives of other men and women — it has a modesty in public recognition of their lives and deeds. It is no mecca of the plaque-hunter; and other than in the Lander memorial, there are no causes for cricked necks from looking ever upward at the mason's skill.

By their deeds the City's sons shall be remembered, not by inscription or effigy.

John Wolcot, the great English satirist known as Peter Pindar, lived at the Britannia Hotel for several years after his return from Jamaica where he had been the island's physician-general. He satisfied Truro's health needs as a much-respected local doctor; encouraged the brilliant portrait and historical painter, John Opie, to go to London in 1780, where his career was to be capped by his election to the Royal Academy; and satisfied his own literary ability in some seventy poetical pamphlets that both scandalised and delighted by their wit, fluency, audacity and coarseness.

Then there were Truro's own native-born sons: Samuel Foote, comedian; Richard Polwhele, cleric and historian; the brothers Lander, of exploration fame; and General Sir Hussey Vivian, the brilliant military commander of the Peninsular War and of Waterloo.

Foote was born in Truro in 1720 and, after education at Truro Grammar School, made his way to a law student's place in London via Worcester and Oxford. He found the law both dreary and cumbersome against his keen wit, his nimble brain, and the gift of mimicry that alienated him from many of the leading figures of London life at an official level, but made him a sought-after guest at private gatherings.

It was his easy-going manner that turned him into the victim of his own folly and, within a few years of his arrival in London, he had spent his entire fortune on clothes and in entertaining his friends and hangers-on lavishly at the Grecian and Bedford coffee houses.

As an amateur he turned to drama, but upset the established theatre by appearing with a producer blacklisted at Drury Lane, and by his effrontery in not only appearing in Vanbrugh's *Relapse*, but by capping a very poor performance as Lord Foppington with his own version of the epilogue.

He went to Dublin where, for the first time, his new dimension to the theatrical tradition was rewarded by crowded houses. He returned to London and appeared in a series of farces written by, produced by, and starring himself. His success was a threat to the 'legitimate' theatre, and a hastily-conceived Licensing Act of 1737 sought to put an end to satirical productions.

The nimble, legal brain of Samuel Foote soon found a way around this hurdle and, instead of inviting the public to buy tickets for his productions in the Haymarket, he advertised:

'On Saturday afternoon, exactly at twelve o'clock, Mr. Foote begs the favour of his friends to come and drink a dish of chocolate with him, and 'tis hoped there will be a great deal of company and some joyous spirits. He will endeavour to make the afternoon as diverting as possible. Tickets to be had for this entertainment at George's Coffee House, Temple Bar, without which no one will be admitted.

N.B., Sir Dilbury Diddle will be there, and Lady Betty Frisk has absolutely promised.

The advertisement did the trick. Curiosity was aroused and the tickets were rapidly sold.

When the curtain rose, Foote walked onto the stage and made an apology. Due to the numbers of his 'friends' who had arrived, he said, there would be some slight delay in making sufficient chocolate. While they waited, they might perhaps care to watch him training some young actors and actresses for a stage performance. The audience stayed, the show went on, the chocolate was served, and Samuel Foote had driven yet another coach and horses through an attempt to curtail his activities while remaining strictly within the law.

In 1747 he invited his 'friends' to 'tea at 6.30', in 1748 to 'chocolate in Ireland', and then to 'an auction of pictures'. For almost twenty years he toured England, Scotland and Ireland with a succession of plays poking fun at everyone in authority, including the Church of England and the Methodists. Before producing probably his best play, *The Minors*, with its satire on the nonconformists, Foote sent the script to the Archbishop of Canterbury for editing, undertaking to remove or alter anything that was unacceptable. Seeing mental pictures of a playbill including the phrase 'as corrected and approved by his Grace the Archbishop of Canterbury', the Archbishop returned the manuscript unread.

In 1766, Foote had what even he, with his gift of satire, would have regarded as a lucky break. He visited the home of Lord Mexborough. In an attempt to amuse other guests, his host persuaded him to mount a frisky horse. Foote was thrown and his leg badly broken. With great courage he demanded an immediate amputation.

His host and fellow guests were so impressed by his attitude to the misfortune that they had so unwittingly caused that they persuaded the authorities to allow him to open a theatre in the Haymarket, with permission to produce and perform plays of his choice from 14 May to 14 September each year. It proved to be a double-edged olive branch, for the libels and innuendo continued, Foote often being harangued by friends of his victims as the productions were actually going on.

On 21 October 1777, he died suddenly while passing through Dover on his way to France to take a holiday on medical advice. Fittingly to the memory of one who had contributed so much gaiety and wit across the footlights, he was buried by torchlight, on the night of 3 November, in the west cloister of Westminster Abbey.

Perhaps the finest tribute to the life and skill of Samuel Foote was that of Dr Samuel Johnson: 'Having no good opinion of the fellow I was resolved not to be pleased, and it is very difficult to please a man against his will. I went on eating my dinner pretty sullenly, affecting not to mind him. But the dog was so very comical that I was obliged to lay down my knife and fork, throw myself back upon my chair, and fairly laugh it out. No, sir, he was irresistible.'

Six years before Foote lost his leg, Truro acquired another famous son, Richard Polwhele. Like Foote, Polwhele was also educated at Truro Grammar School; like Opie, he was encouraged by John Wolcot, by way of some candid criticism. Reading a poem of the then twelve-year-old, Wolcot told him — in 1772 — that he would only succeed as a writer if he would drop his 'damned epithets'.

Polwhele accepted the advice and, at the age of seventeen, published his first volume of poems anonymously merely attributing them to being by 'a young gentleman of Truro School'. This drew the scathing retort of a reviewer that 'the master of that school should have kept it in manuscript'.

Polwhele, with vanity singed, read civil law at Christ Church, Oxford, but left the university without taking a degree, to enter the Church of England, returning to Truro in 1806 as curate of Kenwyn. He was a prolific writer, churning out an endless stream of poetry, essays, theological works, literary chronicles and parochial surveys of Cornish history.

'His fame', it was said, 'has been marred by a fatal fluency of composition.' In attractive style, he worked for many years on detailed histories of Devon and Cornwall, but his work was so lengthy and ponderous that various friends who had promised to sponsor his works either withdrew their offers or else wrote books of their own in far less time. Possibly an eye on the clock rather than an eye on the pen would have earned greater financial rewards for one of Cornwall's foremost historians.

When he died in Truro on 12 March, 1838, at the age of seventy eight, Richard Polwhele left behind him an invaluable contribution to Cornwall's heritage and one that will, perhaps, never be equalled.

Following in the path of Foote and Polwhele through the classrooms of Truro Grammar School, was Richard Hussey Vivian, to be created the first Baron Vivian in 1841 in recognition of his services to the nation as both soldier and politician. Again, like Foote and Polwhele, Vivian was educated for a profession he was not to follow. At the age of eighteen he veered away from his articles as a pupil-solicitor and joined an infantry regiment, transferring to the cavalry in 1798. Ten years later, in command of the 7th Light Dragoons, he joined Sir John Moore's forces and was involved in the retreat from Corunna, his unit constantly forming the rearguard. On one occasion, accompanied only by one sergeant, he rounded up some six hundred straggling infantrymen who had been thrown into disarray by a French cavalry attack; regrouped them; and led them immediately into a very successful counterattack.

For his gallantry and leadership in the Peninsular War, he received the rarely awarded Gold Medal for his successes at Sahagun and Benavente.

In 1812 he was promoted to full Colonel and equerry to the Prince Regent. Within a further eighteen months he had returned to Spain, this time to command the 10th and 14th Light Dragoons. After more successful campaigns he was again promoted and entered 1814 as Commander of a crack division composed of the 18th Light Dragoons and the German Hussars. After fighting his way through Spain, he helped capture Bordeaux and then went on to link up with Wellington for the advance on Toulouse.

Wellington recorded: 'Vivian made a most gallant attack upon a superior body of the enemy's cavalry at Crois d'Orade, and took about one hundred prisoners, gave us possession of an important bridge over the Ers, by which it was necessary to pass to attack the enemy's position. Colonel Vivian was unfortunately wounded upon this occasion, and I am afraid I shall lose his services for some time.'

Within twelve months, Vivian was back in Europe — this time as Colonel Sir Richard Hussey Vivian, Knight Commander of the Most Noble Order of the Bath, commanding the 10th and 18th Light Dragoons and the 12th Hussars of the German Legion, composing the 17th Brigade. It was in this post that, yet again, he found himself in a historic battle. This time it was Waterloo. After using the sight of his cavalry to give extra heart to the British infantry, Vivian exposed his men to shot, shell and musketry to draw the French fire away from other British troops. Then, at the head of his horsemen, he led a successful attack on the enemy, all the time concealing the fact that his right hand was useless as a legacy of the wounds of a year before. He put the French to flight and chased them for as long and as far as daylight allowed.

His honours included a mention in despatches; the thanks of both Houses of Parliament; a knighthood from the Court of Hanover; the Austrian Order of Maria; and the Russian Order of St Vladimir. His most prized possession was, however, yet to come. After Waterloo, his soldiers had been awarded prize-money for French horses and equipment captured at the battle. In a gift of admiration and affection, they all contributed to buy him a silver trumpet and banner.

From 1820 to 1825 he was Member of Parliament for Truro, but returned to the Army as Inspector-General of Cavalry in the first of a series of senior staff posts that were to continue until 1837 when he became Member of Parliament for East Cornwall, which he represented until the creation of his peerage in 1841 — just twelve months before his death in Germany in 1842.

In typical modesty, it was his own request that he be buried in Truro in simple fashion. The wishes were respected, and Cornwall's mourning at the death of one of her greatest military sons was restricted to the tolling of church bells and the flying of flags at half mast.

Of another Truronian, it was to be written that in the brief life-span of thirty one years, from 1781 to 1812, 'his is the one heroic name which adorns the annals of the Church of England from the days of Elizabeth to our own'.

Henry Martyn was the son of a working miner who, by self-discipline and study, had earned his way from the mines of Gwennap to the post of head clerk for a Truro merchant. Henry was a sickly boy who suffered from consumption. At the age of twenty-two he was ordained, but entered the missionary service and went to India in 1806. In the daytime he worked tirelessly among the natives. He learned their dialect and spent his non-pastoral time either studying new languages or in translating the New Testament into Hindustani.

Although he was liked and respected by the Indians, he was often threatened with violence and must have endured, in India, the same difficulties and disappointments that Wesley had encountered in Cornwall but a few short years before.

In 1810 he completed his massive work of translation, and started the second great task — this time of presenting the New Testament in Persian — while, at the same time, preparing a Hindustani version of the prayer book. Taxed and weakened both physically and mentally, Martyn set out, in 1811, to visit Persia with his New Testament and then to go on to Arabia to work on a translation in Arabic. On his journeys he found that he was the first English clergyman that many Mohammedans had met. He spent time and energy that he could ill-afford in discussing Christianity with all those willing to listen.

At Tabriz, in Persia, he tried to present a New Testament in Persian to the Shah. The Shah refused to accept it but, after Martyn had fallen ill with a serious fever, not only changed his mind, but requested the British Ambassador to take it to St Petersburg to be printed and put into circulation.

His work accomplished in Persia, Martyn set off for Constantinople. When he reached Tokat, in Turkey, a combination of fatigue, fever and plague overcame him and he died there.

Although Henry Martyn died among strangers, he was buried in the Armenian cemetery with all the honours usually kept for archbishops, to the tribute of Sir James Stephen: 'While other apostolic men either quitted or were cast out of their communion, Henry Martyn, the learned and the holy, translating the Scriptures in his solitary bungalow at Dinapore, or preaching to a congregation of five hundred beggars, or refuting the Mohammedan doctors at Shiraz, is the bright exception.'

Had he not become an explorer, Richard Lander might well have made a good missionary. His qualities would have suited either calling. He had great intellect, a strong constitution, muscular power, a cheerful disposition, an open face and good manners. He first saw the light of day in 1804 at an inn named the Fighting Cocks, later renamed the Dolphin, and now without a trace other than through a modest plaque on an uninspiring wall on the original site.

In 1817 he went to the West Indies, but was sent home suffering from yellow fever. Wanderlust stayed with him and, in 1823 he visited the Cape Colony and fell in love with Africa. His enthusiasm knew no bounds, and when Captain Clapperton set off on journeys of exploration through West Africa in 1827, Lander went as well — although turning down chances of joining better-paid expeditions to South America.

It was with heavy heart that Richard Lander returned to London, in 1828 with news of Clapperton's death. Entrusted with Clapperton's reports, Lander published an account of their joint travels so authoritatively that, in 1830, he was offered a payment of £100 per annum to his wife during his absence, plus a similar sum for himself on his return, if he would undertake an exploration of the course and the termination of the River Niger.

He needed no urging, and took with him his younger brother, John, who was even prepared to take part in the epic journey without any offer of pay. By canoe, and on foot, they followed the Niger. Not only were there the difficulties and dangers of the river and the river bank to be faced, but there were other perils as well. At one point they were attacked by natives and their stores plundered while the members of the expedition were beaten up. The king of another territory held them as hostages until a ransom was paid. There were, too, the problems of illness and fatigue. John picked up an infection

71

that was to lead to his death some nine years later.

In spite of the difficulties they succeeded in their task. In 1832, Richard Lander returned to the land of the Niger, this time at the request of some Liverpool merchants who wanted to use the mighty river as a trade route into Central Africa. Equipped with two steamers and a third ship carrying coal and other goods, the expedition accomplished much of its mission and the three ships went back to Fernando Po for fresh supplies while Lander went on with a small party for some further exploration. Near Ingiamma they were ambushed by some hostile Brass River natives, and in a brief skirmish Lander was hit in the thigh by a musket ball. As it could not be extracted, the party went back to Fernando Po. Although Lander was given immediate treatment, the wound was more serious than at first recognised, and he died there in February 1834, at the early age of thirty.

Within twelve months, Truro had raised sufficient money, by public subscription, to commission a statue by the Cornish sculptor, Nevill Northey Burnard, 'to the discoveries of our justly-celebrated townsman in Africa'. Although the foundation stone was laid in 1835, work on the fluted Doric column was slow and received an unexpected setback when, in May 1836, the entire structure collapsed. Ironically, the incident occurred while experts were testing the site for safety following a slight subsidence. Work was resumed, Burnard's stone explorer was hoisted into place, and Richard Lander began the tireless vigil over the rivers Allen and Kenwyn that has continued ever since.

'GENTEEL HOUSES
AND COURTEOUS MANNERS'

Nobody with anything approaching a fair mind can deny the accuracy and justification of the many glowing descriptions in words with which Truro has been painted through many hundreds of years.

John Leland wrote, in the mid-1530s, of a small community lying between two brooks.

Fifty years later, John Norden described 'a pretty compacted towne, well peopled and wealthye marchauntes . . . but ther is not a towne in the weste part of the Shyre more comendable for neatnes of buyldinges; nor more discomendable for Pryde of the people.'

Truro, it seemed, was rather conceited regarding its appearance, its success and its growth.

At the beginning of the nineteenth century, the Revd Richard Warner found a 'gay and elegant' town. 'For extent, regularity and beauty, it may properly be denominated the metropolis of Cornwall. Here all the modes of polished life are visible, in genteel houses, elegant hospitality, fashionable apparel, and courteous manners.'

Not to be outwritten, a later visitor wrote: 'Truro is the largest, cleanest, best built, and best regulated town in Cornwall. Its principal streets are wide and granite paved, and have streams of clear water ever flowing through their side channels. Its houses, for the most part are stone fronted and substantial.'

On the land on which the Lander statue now stands, there was 'a convenient and healthy barracks, for three or four hundred horse soldiers, and near them on a spot equally advantageous, a noble Infirmary, supported by voluntary subscriptions, erected for the reception of those unfortunate miners who experience the various accidents to which their dangerous employment is peculiarly liable.'

The extreme width of modern-day Boscawen Street stems from the fact that it was once split down the middle by a Middle Row containing, among other things, a Market Hall. When the old building was demolished more than a century ago, a stone dating back to 1615 was incorporated in the new municipal buildings and City hall, bearing the reminder to traders that he 'who seeks to find eternal treasure must use no guile in weight or measure'.

The existing City hall was built in 1845, to the designs of Christopher Eales and based on the style of the Italian Renaissance, giving the centre of Truro — on a sunny day — a truly Mediterranean feeling.

If picture post cards existed in 1856, then no doubt many featuring this fine building were posted in one of Cornwall's first two pillar boxes which appeared in Lemon Street and Frances Street in time for the 1856 Christmas mail. Although they were intended as a convenience for the public, they had to endure an inaugural rough ride as receptacles for stones, litter and even cigar ends from those who did not understand their true purpose!

Although Truro was a well-integrated town, the records of 1883 would seem to suggest that, residentially, there were streets in which the workers lived, and streets for the wealthy.

The beautiful Walsingham Place, for instance, housed a publican, an insurance agent, a dressmaker, a fruiterer, a law clerk, a cabman, a gardener, a coachbuilder and a hop merchant. Charles Street was home to a mason, a labourer, a chimney sweep, a bargeman, an ostler, a baker, a shoemaker, a mariner, a painter, a pensioner, a brushmaker and a lime-burner.

Kenwyn Street accommodated a better social inter-mix of a box and trunk maker, a publican, a music teacher, a tea merchant and a warehouseman. In the upper-crust area, dignified Princes Street was the domain of bankers, solicitors, dentists, surgeons, shipowners and accountants.

Princes Street was named after the Prince Regent, and contained some of Truro's most fascinating and impressive buildings. William Pitt was a frequent visitor at the home of one of Truro's MPs, Henry Rosewarne, who once lived there in Great House. The massive Mansion House, now accommodating offices, provided a Bath stone frontage to the comfortable home of 'Guinea-a-minute Daniell' — Thomas Daniell — who amassed great wealth from his mining empire at St Agnes. Next to the Mansion House was the birthplace of Henry Martyn.

Few towns can surpass the elegant pathway to prosperity symbolised by Lemon Street, its houses as attractive and stunning today as when they were built in Georgian times, and named — in 1795 — after the great local merchant, Mr Lemon. Although obviously and outwardly a scene of great prosperity, it is worth recalling that, when mining collapsed, Lemon Street saw as many fortunes lost as had ever been made from behind its solid and gracious stonework.

High Cross still retains traces of the Assembly Rooms dating back to 1772, the lofty and beautiful pedimented façade ornamented with its terracotta medallions of Shakespeare and Garrick. Where typewriters now clatter and filing cabinets groan in modern offices, the Assembly Rooms attracted the sparkle of theatrical performances, the wisdom of learned lecturers, and the perfumes, the silks and satins, and the music associated with functions, at which the socially-important danced the night away.

Of more modern construction is the fascination-crammed granite-fronted County Museum of the Royal Institution of Cornwall, a disdainful yard or two back from the more general building line of River Street, but giving lie to the bald generalisation that most museums are like icebergs. It houses a collection of every aspect of industry, culture and discovery that can be brought together to keep Cornwall's past vibrantly alive.

The Royal Institution of Cornwall dates back to 1818, when it was created as the 'Cornwall Literary and Philosophical Society for the diffusion of science and promotion of literature. In 1821 it was designated 'Royal' when King George IV became its patron at the commencement of a long and unbroken link with the Crown. Thirteen years later, in 1834, the Royal Institution moved to a permanent home in Union Place, amassing — in the process — a large number of exhibits associated with the various scientific, historic, educational and cultural lectures given to members.

By the early 1900s it was obvious that the collection had become every bit as important as the academic work of the Royal Institution, and it was decided — in 1906 — to make the museum generally available to the public and, at the same time, to move to a more appropriate setting. River Street was earmarked but, due to the war, the formal opening had to be delayed until the visit of the Prince of Wales in 1919.

Since then the museum has flourished in a unique partnership between the Royal Institution of Cornwall, as sponsors, and local government as grant-paying supporters, and can boast among its many important attractions, the finest collection of minerals to be found anywhere outside the Royal Geological Museum of London.

Many of Truro's fine buildings were, no doubt, controversial —

even futuristic — when they were designed, and the spirit of architectural innovation is still very much in evidence in the City.

In 1966, Cornwall County Council moved from its former headquarters, in Station Road, to a new base in Treyew Road. If the old building, dating only back to 1912, was a showpiece of the dignified use of granite in the cause of the impressive solidarity of local administration, then the new design of County Architect Alan Groves underlined that it was possible to combine modernity with dignity, and functional needs with attractiveness. With its ornamental pond, courtyard and exciting design, it can claim to be one of Truro's most exciting buildings.

The reorganisation of local government, in 1974, has given Truro another modern set-piece in the field of council offices. Until that year the City Council operated from the old municipal buildings, with Truro Rural District Council occupying a converted chapel masked by a semi-modern façade, in River Street. The amalgamation of the Truro councils, with those of Falmouth and Penryn as the new Carrick District Council created the problems of administering a population of seventy-two thousand people. Courageously, but controversially, Carrick decided to build a challenging new centre in one of Truro's oldest areas, Pydar Street. Only time will pass the verdict as to whether the new buildings were masterpieces of taste, or architectural irresponsibility on a massive scale.

'EXCEEDING MAGNIFICAL'

A bust of John Wesley by the Cornish sculptor, Nevill Northey
Burnard, might indeed seem a strange presence in the private chapel
of former Bishops of Truro, at Kenwyn, and in what is now part of
Truro Cathedral School.

While it is true that it is a copy of that carved by Burnard for the
meeting house at Altarnun, the connection between Wesley and
Truro is one of the most fascinating of his life. At first glance it
seems that the great preacher ignored the town between 1746 and
1761, other than in one or two private visits to the home of the then
vicar of Kenwyn, the Revd Richard Milles. There are many accounts
of his having preached on the fringes of Truro, but few indeed of his
having been active within the limits of the town's parishes.

In August 1755, Wesley wrote of 'riding through Truro'; in September of 1762, of standing in the street 'at a small distance from the
market'; and only in September 1766, did he write: 'At noon I
preached in Truro.'

The entries for 1755 and 1766 do, however, provide two curious
clues to his having passed through Truro on his journeys to other
parts of Cornwall. The details of August 1755 record that, as he rode
through Truro on his way from St Austell to Redruth: 'one stopped
my horse and insisted on my alighting. Presently two or three more
of Mr. Walker's society came in, and we seemed to have been
acquainted with each other many years; but I was constrained to
break from them.'

It was the same Mr Walker who featured in the entry in Wesley's
journal for 4 September, 1766: 'at noon I preached in Truro. I was in
hopes, when Mr. Walker died, the enmity in those who were called
his people would have died also. But it is not so; they still look upon
us as rank heretics, and will have no fellowship with us.'

Anyone familiar with the work of John Wesley in Cornwall will,
from these extracts, assume that Mr Walker was the leader of a
sect totally opposed to the rigidity of Wesley's preaching and the

fervour of his message. Yet, in fact, the reverse is true.

Mr Walker was the Revd Samuel Walker, curate of St Mary's, Truro, from 1746 to 1761, and who only parted theological company with Wesley since, in his view, the visiting preacher did not go far enough with his warnings to those who strayed from the path of righteousness. There was, indeed, a close bond between the two men. It was out of this respect that Wesley accepted Walker's opinions, and resolved never to preach in Truro while he was there.

Walker was indeed a thorn in the flesh of the established Church. Morally and religiously unbending, he held the conviction — both harsh and uncompromising — that while there could be eternal salvation for those who followed a disciplined life, there would be eternal damnation for those who sinned. He held these views so deeply that on several occasions he even cut short the burial services of those he believed to have been transgressors, and was twice summoned to Exeter for a ticking-off by the Bishop who, at that time, was responsible for both Exeter and Cornwall.

It was Walker's view that Wesley was a 'moderate' in his ministry and that his choice of laymen to preach the message of the nonconformist faith would lead to major problems when some of them turned their sights towards becoming trained and paid ministers. Letters flowed between Walker and both Wesleys, and it seemed that while Charles Wesley was prepared to recognise some of Walker's views, John Wesley's attitude was more one of formal respect than actual acceptance.

It was, however, not John Welsey's task to undermine Walker's status in Truro and his undoubted evangelical brilliance and successes with a populace seeking spiritual direction. That Walker was a zealot is beyond doubt. His successor at St Mary's, the Revd Charles Pye, observed ruefully that: 'My pulpit so stinks of Calvinism that not a century will purge it.'

A purge was hardly necessary, for when Walker died in 1761, his followers left St Mary's and formed their own sect on most demanding lines. Hence it was that, in September 1766, Wesley's hopes that they would turn to more moderate — and hopeful — nonconformity were dashed when he found that Walker's followers regarded his teachings and values as rank heresy.

It took fifteen years for Wesley to eventually overcome the lingering influence of Walker's doctrines and this was rewarded when, in August 1781, he could write of his Truro meeting: 'I have not for many years seen a congregation so universally affected. One would have imagined every one that was present had a desire to save his soul.'

Again, in 1787, Wesley found the Truro preaching-house 'well filled with deeply attentive hearers'.

Despite the influence of Samuel Walker and John Wesley, Truro had long been a place of great religious significance in Cornish history. Long before 1066, Cornwall had enjoyed its own Bishopric, that of St Germans, uniting it with Crediton in 1043, and seeing the united See transferred to Exeter in 1050.

The 'Black Friars' of the Dominican Order arrived in England in 1221 but, by 1259, had established themselves in a friary to the west of the Kenwyn river. It was one of nineteen Cornish churches consecrated by Bishop Bronescombe as he toured Cornwall between 24 September and 25 October that year.

It isn't known when first a church was built on the site now occupied by Truro cathedral, but it is beyond doubt that the Dominicans were not Truro's first ecclesiastical builders. St Mary's church, incorporated in the cathedral, contained portions of the 1259 building. However, when the older structure was demolished, it was found that the 1259 portion contained fragments of masonry and other materials suggesting an even earlier building.

It is worth remembering that churches at Kenwyn and St Clement's were also consecrated in Bishop Bronescombe's energetic tour of 1259; that St John's, at the top of Lemon Street, was founded in 1827; St Paul's, in 1845; and St George's, in 1855. Since 1830, Truro's main Methodist church — regarded by many as 'The Methodist cathedral' — has stood in Union Place, its fifteen hundred seats now providing modern accommodation behind a historic façade.

In terms of modernity, none can equal Truro's new Roman Catholic church. In 1880, the church was described as 'a dilapidated building on a small site which offers little prospect'. From 1884 to 1972, the congregation worshipped in a small church in Dereham Terrace, before moving — in that year — to a breathtakingly beautiful new building in St Austell Street, dedicated to Our Lady of the Portal with St Piran, recalling both the ancient shrine that once stood in the parish of St Clement, and the patron saint of Cornish miners.

Dominating all is the cathedral. In August 1876, an Act of Parliament made provision for the separation of the Archdeaconry of Cornwall from the Diocese of Exeter 'in order that the former might be made a separate Diocese'. It was not an instant decision. In 1847 a similar Bill, favouring Bodmin for the new cathedral, was defeated. In 1860 there was an unsuccessful attempt to recreate the separate diocese of St Germans. That, too, failed, as did another in 1864 which drew the personal view of Mr Gladstone that: 'Bearing in mind the greatly increased facilities recently created of communications by the penny post, and of moving from one part of the country to another, by the railroad, that render it easier now than formerly for a bishop to look after a diocese of large extent, Her Majesty's Government do not think that any sufficient ground at present exists for entertaining the general question of dividing the diocese of Exeter by severing from it the County of Cornwall.'

In June 1876, it was 'leaked' to the then rector of Truro that it was proposed 'in the event of the creation of a Cornish Bishopric' to make the parish church of Truro the cathedral of the diocese, despite the rival claims of Bodmin, St Austell and St Germans. The 'leak' became a deluge. In December 1876, an Order in Council created the See, and Queen Victoria nominated Edward White Benson to be the first Bishop of Truro. He was consecrated in St Paul's cathedral, London, on 25 April 1877, and enthroned in the old parish church of St Mary, Truro, on 1 May 1877. In August 1877, the *London Gazette* recorded: 'The Queen has been pleased by Letters Patent under the Great Seal of the United Kingdom, bearing the date 28th day of August, 1877, to ordain and declare that the borough of Truro, in the county of Cornwall, shall be a City, and shall be called and styled "the City of Truro in the county of Cornwall".'

Dr Benson was undoubtedly a visionary. It was said that he actually saved Cornwall rather than merely founding a diocese. As befitted a man later to become Archbishop of Canterbury, he was committed to the dignity of the church in physical as well as religious terms. It was obvious that the old parish church was in need of repair and that, in any case, it was inadequate to its new role.

In 1872 the then Bishop of Carlisle had predicted that England would never again see the creation of great cathedrals. No-one, he suggested, 'would venture to design a structure such as those which the medieval architects have left us.'

Benson disagreed — and disagreed even more with those who said that even if a cathedral could be designed, the poverty of Cornwall would make it impossible to turn designs and drawings into a constructional reality. He called a 'Grand County Meeting', and was rewarded by an unexpected enthusiasm for his wish not that Truro should merely have a cathedral, but that it should be 'exceeding magnifical', to the glory of God and to the service of Cornwall.

A combination of jingoism, magnetism and dedication overwhelmed the new diocese. Truro would indeed have its cathedral. The Bishop of Carlisle would be proved wrong. Like a phoenix, a new building of faith would arise from the cramped central area of Truro's historic church to dominate the new City.

Enlisted as architect was John Loughborough Pearson. He shared Benson's vision, and set himself the task of building a great cathedral on a tiny site; of embodying hundreds of years of Cornish faith in a new concept; and of creating something 'that will bring people soonest to their knees in inspired worship and the perspectives of eternity'.

Since Truro could not be without a place of worship, Pearson's great design actually incorporated St Mary's as a continuing parish church encompassed by the new building.

Money would indeed be in short supply, so the estimated price was set at £95,000, excluding the three spires and interior fittings. As local materials would be the cheapest, Pearson and his advisors scoured the quarries of Truro, Chacewater, St Columb, Lostwithiel and Redruth, before deciding on Mabe granite for the exterior, and stone from St Stephen's for the inside.

By the early months of 1880, the area from which the cathedral would grow was being cleared. Down came houses and an inn; streets were blocked off; machinery and scaffolding began to accumulate. On 20 May, 1880, the foundation stones were laid by the Prince of Wales as Grand Master of Freemasons, in the company of 'most of the Nobility, Gentry and Clergy of the County, about 2,000 Freemasons from all parts of England, and an immense concourse of people. Such a splendid gathering has never before been witnessed in the county, and so well conducted was every detail in the day's proceedings as to cause His Royal Highness to express his unqualified surprise and approbation, and to intimate his intention of repeating his visit. The arches, decorations, and illuminations were magnificent, whilst the weather, like the county greeting, was right royal.'

The demolition of the old St Mary's church began three months later and the whole building was removed except the south aisle, the last service being that of harvest festival, on 11 October 1880. On the following Sunday, services were held in the chapel of St Mary's burial ground but, by Christmas, worship had been transferred to a temporary wooden church costing £450 which acted as Truro's cathedral until it was possible to use the first parts of the new building in 1887 following the consecration of the choir and transepts.

It was in the 'wooden cathedral', on Christmas Eve, 1880, that Bishop Benson introduced the famous service of Nine Lessons that, although created for the people of Truro, has now become an international religious festival.

The wooden building was eventually sold, in 1888, and taken to Redruth for use as a shoe factory.

In 1887, the Prince of Wales returned to Truro, this time for the consecration by Dr Benson who, in 1883, had moved to Canterbury to be followed, as second Bishop of Truro, by the Revd George Howard Wilkinson, formerly vicar of St Peter's, Eaton Square, London. The Prince sailed into Falmouth aboard the Royal Yacht, and travelled to Truro by special train.

There was another Royal visit in 1903 by a different Prince of Wales — this time the future King George V — who came to Truro for the dedication of the nave and the naming of the central tower the Victoria Tower after his grandmother. After a further seven years, the two western towers were dedicated to the memory of King Edward VII and Queen Alexandra.

In just thirty years, the dream of Benson, enthusiastically continued by Bishop Wilkinson, and followed through by Bishops Gott and Stubbs had become a reality, Truro's great place of worship earned its completed place among the greatest of Britain's religious buildings. Among the bishops honoured at Truro is Frederick Temple, 93rd Archbishop of Canterbury, who, according to a modest memorial, 'as Bishop of Exeter, worked so hard in the restoration of their ancient Bishopric to the people of Cornwall'.

'VENDED IN PLENTY'

The majority of Cornish towns have been so associated with the specific industries of tin, clay, fishing, agriculture or tourism, that the result has been that they have become identified as 'one-job' towns with, perhaps, an undue emphasis on one occupation. Other than as a spell as a tin centre, and as a tin coinage town until as late as 1838, Truro has been very much a commercial centre rather than an industrial one, and has flirted with Cornwall's shoppers and consumers rather than having a more specific link with industry.

Its attitude to trade through the centuries is as true now as it was, when it was written — two centuries ago — that 'all the commodities necessary to the life of men are vended in great plenty'.

If one calling is, perhaps, slightly more in evidence than the others, then it is agriculture. Farmers needed to buy and sell, so markets were established both for livestock and for produce; farm kitchens needed crockery, so Truro acquired a pottery; ploughs and harrows were the tools of the trade, and Truro provided them; if local fairs and celebrations needed gingerbreads, then Truro made them; and if people needed cars and tractors, then Truro sold them.

But it was to the shopper that Truro provided the greatest appeal. It seemed that shopkeepers were tireless in seeking new goods to satisfy new demands; and that traders and professional men were not slow in offering the latest developments or the newest goods and fads.

In 1811, a Truro dentist-surgeon could provide real and artificial teeth, or real teeth — from one to a full set — in artificial gums; teeth grafted onto old stumps; gold teeth set in gold gums; and a service to sufferers of toothache whereby 'the most dangerous stumps' could be drawn 'without the use of a surgeon's implement'.

By 1880, registered traders included bellows-makers, cloggers, copper-plate printers, cricketing outfitters, feather cleaners, illuminators, manure merchants, music warehouses, pipe makers, stay and corset makers, scourers, tanners and woolstaplers.

As an introduction to what was to become early closing day, the leading drapers closed at mid-afternoon on Fridays in order to give their staff 'an opportunity for open air recreation'. The staff, however, were little better off since closing time on Wednesday and Saturday evenings was then fixed at nine o'clock.

If people fell ill, then one chemist could offer air cushions, enema syringes, ice-bags and knee caps, and special waters for Gravel and Gout. From his shop in King Street, Mr Ivey sold 'The Hygiene Boot', whilst running the additional service of a Registry Office for Servants.

Mr Cock, the appropriately-named plumber of East Bridge Street, fitted hot water systems; fixed water closets; and re-tinned copper stewpans 'all on the most reasonable terms'. At the turn of the century, Mr John Powning, paper merchant, asked the public: 'Why send to Bristol and Plymouth for wrapping papers, etc., when these can be obtained at these premises at a few minutes' notice?'

A trades directory of 1905 reminded the people of Truro that they could buy 'Medallions of Truro Cathedral, as specially made for HRH the Prince of Wales, in silver, from 6d (2½p) each'. Pandering to the growing preoccupation of ladies with their outward appearance, Mr Carter, a chemist of Lemon Street, marketed Glycion, 'so efficacious in rendering the skin delicately soft, smooth and white. It removes and prevents all roughness, redness, chaps, sun-burns, tan-spots, and all other blemishes of the skin occasioned by hard water, cold winds, frost, exposure to the sun, sea-bathing, etc. N.B. All drugs and chemicals used in this establishment are of the best quality and tested purity.'

The Newham Coal Supply Company provided and delivered 'the best Parlour and Kitchen coals, all guaranteed perfectly dry and of best quality'.

Motorists could visit the County Coach Factory, in Tabernacle Street, to take advantage of 'the latest plant for putting on all kinds of rubber tyres, including the Secretfix wired-on tyre which is guaranteed not to open at the joints, and the wires not to cut through the sides'.

For those who fancied the printed word, Messrs Netherton & Worth offered (perhaps rather pompously) the 'best written' books 'in the Cornish provincial dialect'; a call to the Truro Steam Laundry, 'by written post card', would bring their van to your door; while in surely the most baffling sales slogan of all time, Messrs Oscar

84

Blackford advertised: 'You can post Truro with Blackford's Stations. You cannot post Truro without them', presumably referring to the many poster-sites and advertising hoardings it held throughout the City.

If so many claims and counter-claims and so many honest and earnest traders bewildered the customer with their extravagant claims, there was no relief in merely shopping where a trader exhibited the 'By Appointment' Royal Warrant. It seemed that almost everyone was appointed to someone of note. So, in a masterpiece of ingenuity, Mr W.G. Goodfellow, maker of Ronal Jam, modestly claimed that he was, uniquely, 'the youngest Royal Warrant holder in Great Britain'.

There is one interesting sideline to Truro's prosperity. While many towns, in the mid-1800s, were establishing cottage industries of one form or another, the Truro Society for the Encouragement of Industry was created to provide both work and money for the poor, working from their own homes. In 1850, the Society was told that almost four thousand garments had been made during the year from materials costing £115.1s.4d (£115.6p). The profit on this was £39.15s.10d (£39.79), and all but 6s.4d (32p) was passed on for charitable purposes.

There was much activity, too, in the licensed trade, both from the point of view of beer sales and in the provision of accommodation for tourists, travellers and commercial representatives. The Royal Hotel provided 'additional comfort and convenience so that Tourists and Mining Gentlemen may also make this a home whilst in the county'.

The Hicks family moved from the art of the blacksmith and the wheelwright to the sale of bicycles, and then to motor cars, in a long progression that took them from River Street, in 1876, to City Road, and then to Lemon Quay in 1977, to notch up a '100 not out' in the field of personal transport. James Julian moved from cabinet-making and upholstery, in 1836, to found what was to become — as John Julian & Co. Ltd — one of Cornwall's biggest firms of house removers, furnishers and estate agents. Then there were James Jenkin Smith and W.J. Criddle who combined their skills and their trading expertise, to become Criddle & Smith, 'Upholsterers to HRH The Prince of Wales in Cornwall', and ultimately to King Edward VII and King George V.

Gill, Roberts, Rice and Webb were family names associated, until the 1950s and the 1960s with the drapery trade in its finest traditions of quality and respect for its customers. In the food sector, W.J. Kemp and Amos Jennings are still names recalled with pride and affection.

The Blewett family, with their huge bakeries and their shops that have always spilled the true aroma of new-baked bread into the streets of the City, prospered. So, too, did the Furniss family with their faultless biscuits, sweets, and Cornish gingerbreads; the Carveth family with their stationery business; and the Treseders with their horticultural interests.

These families, and their businesses, were so much a part of Truro that even though their shops have now disappeared in many cases, their names are still mentioned with pride even by younger Truronians weaned on the experience and respect of their parents and grandparents.

Truro today is a mixture of the old and the new. Multiple stores, bitterly fought until after the second World War, act as a magnet to one of Cornwall's greatest proliferations of small, independent traders. But above all, Truro — on the trading record of many centuries — is a town of unassuming success. It doesn't need banners to proclaim its justified confidence in itself. It does not have rows of empty shops, their fronts boarded-up to act as a belated barrier to financial ruin. It is a City based on private enterprise and on a long and proud record of answering the needs of the customer both with competitiveness and courtesy, making a mockery of the all-too-common belief that courtesy costs time and hits profits.

Perhaps this tradition is something that has stemmed from the very real and lasting concern that the City has provided in looking after its workers. In 1868, for instance, although bye-laws were introduced to stop apprentices and errand boys frequenting the Working Men's Club 'during their masters' time', the Club not only provided billiards, skittles and bagatelle for its five hundred members, but also had a very popular library which issued over eight hundred books in just one period of six months. Prosperity was being used to encourage culture.

To offset the attractions of alcohol, the Truro Coffee Tavern Co. Ltd, operated in High Cross, 'to be as attractive as possible for all sections of the Temperance Public, providing good articles in good style at a moderate rate'.

It was a continuing battle, abstinence versus alcohol, for Truro's

1883 population of nine thousand could be tempted by any of the proprietors of three breweries, nine beer houses, seven wine, spirit, ale or porter merchants, or any one of thirty seven licensed inns or hotels.

In living memory, beer was brought to Truro by barge, as was the malt for local brewing. The barge was also used for deliveries to waterside pubs. One day the Devenish barge suddenly disappeared into the depths of the Truro river — it had sunk — and all that could be seen were the head and shoulders of the bargeman, Bill Dunn, above the water.

Bill died only a few years ago. He had delivered beer for Devenish on foot, by bicycle, horse, steam, petrol and diesel lorries. He was a great man with horses and, at his funeral, it seemed quite fitting that whilst mourners formed three sides of the square around his grave, the fourth side was completed by a pair of horses who came and cropped the top of the nearby hedge.

In trade and in commerce, in the controversy between beer and abstinence, Truro has been a gentle place with a keen love of the past, but the ability to anticipate change . . . and to accept it.

BOOKS CONSULTED

C. Noall, *A History of Cornish Mail and Stage Coaches*
                                               (D. Bradford Barton Ltd)

W.J. Burley, *City of Truro, 1877-1977*   (Oscar Blackford Ltd)

John Norden, *Description of Cornwall*   (Frank Graham)

R.M. Barton, *Life in Cornwall*   (D. Bradford Barton Ltd)

H.L. Douch, *Old Cornish Inns*   (D. Bradford Barton Ltd)

H. Miles Brown, *The Church in Cornwall*   (Oscar Blackford Ltd)

Richard Pearse, *The Ports and Harbours of Cornwall*   (H.E. Warne)

Donald Brook, *The Romance of the English Theatre*   (Rockliff)

John Pearce, *The Wesleys in Cornwall*   (D. Bradford Barton Ltd)

Henry Lloyd, *Truro Cathedral*   (Photo Precision Ltd)

The author has also referred to files of *The West Briton*, and to various Truro official guide books covering the years 1883-1978.

ACKNOWLEDGMENTS

The Author would like to record his thanks to Mr John Crowther for his assistance in obtaining many of the illustrations; to Mr H.L. Douch for identifying them by date and place; and to the Royal Institution of Cornwall for permission to use material from their collection.

He is grateful to the staff of the County Library, Truro, for the availability of certain books and pamphlets for research purposes.

He thanks Kerry Mudd for artistic advice, and Saul Mudd for his enthusiasm, tolerance and company on photographic missions.

But above all, he thanks Mr John Protheroe, formerly of Truro Cathedral School, for initiating him into the pleasures of history and for, perhaps more than anyone else, creating the wish to write this book.

OTHER BOSSINEY TITLES BY DAVID MUDD

CORNWALL & SCILLY PECULIAR

David Mudd uses his perceptive eye and his pride of all things Cornish to write entertainingly, at times with humour, but always affectionately, of some of the people, events, values and beliefs that create the background to Cornwall's strange and compelling charm.

". . . one of the most important Cornish titles produced by Bossiney . . ."

(The Cornishman)

48 photographs
ISBN 0 906456 11 8
                                    Price £1.00

DOWN ALONG CAMBORNE & REDRUTH

With a mine of magnificent old photographs and some present day ones by Ray Bishop, the local MP charts the history of the two towns from the 12th century to the present. "I like a good meaty story," he says, "that has an accent on the curious, the bizarre, or even the macabre."

"Spicey but informative . . . extremely good value . . ."

Robert Jobson (Camborne-Redruth Packet)

44 photographs
ISBN 0 906456 03 7
                                    Price 95p

THE FALMOUTH PACKETS

The story of the mail packets — an overseas service — and the men who ran it to make Falmouth famous and prosperous. 25 illustrations bring back to life a story that ended before the camera arrived.

". . . the only history of the Falmouth Packet ships to be written in this century . . . vivid and lively . . ."

Enid Thompson, (Western Morning News)

25 illustrations   **Price 75p**
ISBN 0 906456 04 5

CORNISH SEA LIGHTS

In this, his Bossiney hat-trick, David Mudd pilots his readers afloat and aloft with the story of notable Cornish lighthouses, lightships, designers and builders in a factual account of courage, enterprise, danger and intrigue.

". . . will be enjoyed by all those who relish tales of triumph over adversity . . ."

(The West Briton)

29 illustrations and map   **Price 75p**
ISBN 0 906456 01 0

91

ALSO AVAILABLE

SUPERNATURAL IN CORNWALL

by Michael Williams 24 photographs. Price £1.50.

"... a book of fact, not fiction ... covers not only apparitions, and things that go bump in the night, but also witchcraft, clairvoyancy, spiritual healing, even wart charming ..."
Jenny Myerscough on BBC

"Serious students of ghost-hunting will find a fund of locations."
Graham Danton on Westward TV

CHARLES, DUKE OF CORNWALL

by Michael Williams 30 photographs. Price 75p.

"This, the first ever publication about Prince Charles in his role as Duke of Cornwall is full of character and interest. There are recollections of people who have met him, accounts of visits to the Westcountry, his service training in the south-west, at Dartmouth and Yeovilton; fascinating facts and figures about the Duchy of Cornwall which stretches across six counties and has made the Prince one of the wealthiest young men in the world. A story that will appeal to all West-country people — and Royalists everywhere."
David Clarke
Cornish Life

MAKING POLDARK

by Robin Ellis. Over 60 photographs. Price 75p.
The inside story of the popular BBC TV series.

"... an interesting insight into the making of the TV series ..."
Camborne Redruth Packet

"It is a 'proper job', as they say, and a credit to all concerned."
Archer in Cornwall Courier

POLDARK COUNTRY

by David Clarke. Over 40 photographs.   Price 75p.
Published in conjunction with Cornish Life Magazine: fascinating facts about the Cornish past, locations used for the TV series and interviews with Winston Graham and the cast.

MY CORNWALL

A personal vision of Cornwall by eleven writers living and working in the county: Daphne du Maurier, Ronald Duncan, James Turner, Angela du Maurier, Jack Clemo, Denys Val Baker, Colin Wilson, C.C. Vyvyan, Arthur Caddick, Michael Williams and Derek Tangye with reproductions of paintings by Margo Maeckelberghe and photographs by Bryan Russell. Price 95p.

"An ambitious collection of chapters."
The Times, London

THE LIZARD

by Jill Newton 75p

"... captures so well the magical atmosphere of the place, full of legend, restless green seas, crying curlews and sheltered byways ... deserves a place on the shelf of any serious collector of Cornish books."
Pamela Leeds, The Western Evening Herald